SIX KEYS
TO A HAPPY MARRIAGE

Six Keys to a Happy Marriage

● ● ●

A Tyndale Treasure by

TIM LaHAYE

Tyndale House
Publishers, Inc.
Wheaton, Illinois

Six Keys to a Happy Marriage is adapted
from *How to Be Happy Though Married*
by Tim LaHaye, copyright © 1968 by
Tyndale House Publishers, Wheaton, Illinois.

Seventh printing, November 1983

Library of Congress Catalog Card Number 72-84420
ISBN 0-8423-5895-1
Printed in the United States of America

MADE FOR EACH OTHER

Marriage can be the most happy, or mediocre, or unhappy experience of all life. God designed the opposite sexes to complement each other. He wanted a man and woman to be joined in marriage so they might each give to the other what each one lacked. But these differences that can complement and blend two unique individuals into one can also be incompatibilities that divide and cause separation. Sex and marriage are often referred to as "doing what comes naturally," but evidence that it is not an instinctive relationship is found in the great unhappiness of many married people. The high divorce rate in the United States is one indication of much marital unhappiness.

The daily parts and pieces of marriage do not automatically fall into place as the romantic glamor of Hollywood indicates. Loving and living with your partner takes daily determination and practice —and the giving of oneself for the good of the other.

Since God created man and woman for each other, it follows that the best advice on marriage is in God's Book, the Bible. God planned marriage for man's good: "And the Lord God said, It is not good that the man should be alone; I will make him an help meet for him. . . . And Adam said, This is now bone of my bones, and flesh of my flesh: she shall be called Woman, because she was taken out of Man. Therefore shall a man leave his father and his mother, and shall cleave unto his wife: and they shall be one flesh" (Genesis 2:18, 23-24).

Man was the only creature God created alone in the Garden; all the animals were made male and female and had mates. However, human beings were created in the image of God (Genesis 1:26) and given an eternal soul (Genesis 2:7) and a mere mate was not sufficient for man's emotional and spiritual needs. Thus, God planned for a man and woman to be more than mates—to be *helpmates*. Herein lies the secret of a happy marriage. If two people have only the "mating urge" in common, theirs will always be an inadequate relationship, scarcely more satisfying than the relationship of animals. In order for man to find ultimate happiness in marriage he and his wife must work together to make their mental, spiritual, emotional, and physical differences blend into a harmonious relationship.

A couple starts out their marriage very much in love. Because of their natural differences, which gradually become more and more apparent, conflict comes into their relationship. If they don't learn how to resolve these conflicts their love will be replaced by hostility and animosity, reducing their chance for a happy marriage.

The late Dr. M. R. DeHaan, Bible teacher and medical doctor, stated, "The nearest thing to heaven on this earth is the Christian family and the home where husband and wife and parents and children live in love and peace together for the Lord and for each other. The nearest thing to hell on earth is an ungodly home, broken by sin and iniquity, where parents bicker, quarrel, and separate, and children are abandoned to the devil and all the forces of wickedness."[1]

One of the most common causes of emotionally disturbed people today is the average American home. Instead of experiencing security-building love between their parents, children all too often see and feel the traumas of hostility, hatred, and animosity between the two people they love most: their mother and father. From this hostility children develop emotional insecurity and fears that follow them all through life.

God's plan for home life is different from this general experience. He wants the home to be a haven of love where husband and wife and children live with a sense of security and a feeling of acceptance. With all the turmoil and violence outside the home, everyone needs some place in life where he is surrounded by peace and love. God ordained the home as that place of emotional safety. Everyone who marries wants that kind of home, but a happy home doesn't just happen. It is the result of two things: proper adjustment to each other, and incorporation into daily life of the marriage principles outlined by God in the Bible.

[1]"The Christian Home," by M. R. DeHaan (Grand Rapids Radio Bible Class).

3

The principles in the following pages are the culmination of research and counseling with hundreds of couples before and after marriage. I have seen "miracles" in the lives of the couples who were willing to follow them. These couples have achieved a happy marriage.

Many couples after receiving marital counseling have said, "I wish these instructions were in print so we could go home and study them together." My prayer is that God will use them to help many couples adjust to each other and fill their home with love, warmth, and understanding that will make them "happy though married."

O O O

THE PROBLEMS

Most marriage counselors acknowledge three basic areas of marital adjustment —mental, physical, and spiritual. Proper adjustment in each of these areas is necessary to create a well-rounded marriage. If we were to let a circle represent the total marriage, then each of the three adjustment areas would represent about one-third of the total relationship. Although the age of the couple when married and the length of the marriage are factors which can make one area more important than another, over a lifetime of marriage the three areas are approximately equal in importance. In the twenties the physical may dominate the others, but in the thirties the mental often dominates the physical and spiritual, and from the late thirties on the spiritual usually dominates the others.

These three adjustment areas are always interdependent. It is unusual for couples to have good physical adjustment if they do not have a high degree of mental adjustment. I have known couples whose difficulty in adjusting mentally produced physical maladjustment, but because of their strong spiritual relationship—through faith in Christ—

they were able to make better mental and physical adjustments. The spiritual is potentially the most important because it can radically improve the adjustment in the other two.

The mental adjustment in marriage, while usually the most complex, offers an exciting opportunity for two people to get to know each other deeply. Due to the fact that individuals are prone to be on their best behavior all through courtship, most married couples have tremendous mental adjustments to make. This area of adjustment highlights background differences and encompasses a variety of experiences that require retraining.

In physically adjusting a couple starts out learning a whole new experience. In the spiritual realm they can, through the study of the Word of God, similarly learn a new relationship to each other and to God. But in the mental area each has spent approximately twenty or more years adjusting to other people according to his own pattern. Now they come into marriage, with its responsibilities and natural pressures, and may find that their adjustment patterns to certain experiences are in conflict with their partner's. Therefore, take special note of the golden rule of mental adjustment as found in Philippians 2:3-4:

"Let nothing be done through strife or vainglory; but in lowliness of mind let each esteem other better than themselves. Look not every man on his own things, but every man also on the things of others."

With determination before God to forget yourself and make your partner happy as these verses teach, you cannot help but make wholesome adjustments to the many mental facets of married life. I shall discuss five of the most common problems of mental adjustment.

Finances

Financial adjustment is perhaps the most difficult, partially because most couples have been so dependent upon their parents. The situation is further confused today by both husband and wife working. If the wife has worked prior to marriage and kept her own checking account, it is natural that she may want to do the same afterward. If she is going to work to help her husband finish his education, she may assume the role of breadwinner and look down on her husband rather than recognize that her endeavor is an investment in their lifetime vocation—an investment that will pay lifelong dividends.

Who Should Handle the Money? The answer to this question is far more significant than just dollars and cents. God has stated very clearly in his Word that the man should be the head of the house. This principle produces happiness; violation of the principle produces misery. I have never known a happy henpecked husband, nor have I ever met a happy henpecker. God would never ask a woman to be in subjection to her husband unless it was for her good. A woman will not be lastingly happy unless she is in subjection to her husband.

Why is this important in relationship to finances? Simply because of the truth of an age-old adage, "He that holds the purse strings rules the family." You will find that the treasurer of any organization often has an inordinate consciousness of power. This is particularly true in a family. Whether the wife is a trained bookkeeper and the husband a terrible mathematician has nothing to do with it. The husband should handle the finances in a marriage, particularly for the first seven to ten years.

This does not mean that the wife should not have her area of responsibility. A couple can plan a budget that provides the wife with a set amount for food, household expenses, her miscellaneous needs, and such other things as they agree upon. The husband then should pay the bills, balance the bank account, and be responsible for the overall financial structure. They should not have separate bank accounts; if the wife works she should put her earnings into the family account. Large purchases of furniture, appliances, cars, etc., should be by joint agreement. Anytime one of the partners is opposed to a particular financial investment, it would be far better to wait until there is agreement than to have one defy the other's feelings on the matter.

The Working Wife. It is increasingly popular for wives to work. Many young couples think that getting started in marriage, saving enough to make a down payment on a home, or helping a husband through college are acceptable reasons for a wife to work. This arrangement should only be until children come into the home. However, when a wife works, certain dangers arise that should be considered.

The most important is that if the wife works and keeps her money separate from her husband's, it breeds a feeling of independence and self-sufficiency which God did not intend a married woman to have. This feeling makes it difficult for her to adjust to her husband during the early stages of marriage. I am convinced that one of the reasons young married couples divorce so readily today is because the wife is not economically dependent upon her husband; whenever difficulties and pressures arise she can say, as one young lady said to me, "I don't have to take that kind of thing; I can live by myself!" I always recommend that a joint bank account be kept and that a working wife keep from her paycheck only what she needs for her living and household expenses. Marriage is a joint venture between two people who live as one. It is not two distinct corporations doing business under the same roof.

The second danger to a working wife is that the birth of children is often delayed too long. If you wait until you can afford to have children, you will probably never have them. They are such a source of enrichment and blessing in a family that young people should plan early on having them and work toward that date; otherwise you may cheat yourselves out of the blessing of parenthood and thus be disobedient to God's command that we "... be fruitful, and multiply, and replenish the earth ..." (Genesis 1:28).

Indebtedness. One of the severe problems in many marriages is that within a few weeks after marriage a couple find themselves hopelessly in debt. This financial strain produces tensions and fears that are an unnecessary hindrance to a proper adjustment. Avoid impulse buying; obligate yourselves only for the absolute essentials. Someone has suggested that monthly payments should never exceed ten percent of a couple's income, in addition to automobile and house payments. The wife's attitude toward possessions is very important in the early stages of marriage; she can unconsciously drive her husband to overextend himself in an effort to please her. She should avoid comparisons between the home her father was able to provide and the little apartment and frugal conditions under which she starts marriage. Remember that parents have had twenty years or more in which to accumulate the possessions they enjoy, and in due time you may hope for the same. The wife's patience and joyous acceptance of her husband's financial capabilities are among the ways she can invest in a long-lasting and happy marriage.

Fiscal Responsibility. A responsible fiscal program for the Christian couple was beautifully described by Charlie W. Shedd in "Letters to Karen" (his daughter), published in *Reader's Digest*, January, 1966, in which he gave this motto: "Give ten percent, save ten percent, and spend the rest with thanksgiving and praise!"

As a Christian couple, start out immediately securing God's blessing on your family finances according to Malachi 3:3-11 by giving him one-tenth of your income. You can literally accomplish more financially with God's blessing on the expenditure of 90 percent than you can the 100 percent without God's blessing. I have never known a couple that was not blessed by tithing. ". . . prove me now herewith, saith the Lord of hosts, if I will not open you the windows of heaven, and pour you out a blessing, that there shall not be room enough to receive it" (Malachi 3:10).

By saving the second ten percent, you will find it possible to pay cash for some of the items you need without expensive interest charges and the pressure of payments. If you do not start out your marriage with these two practices, you may find it difficult to start later. However, it is not impossible. Give God the tithe and trust him to guide you through your financial problems. He never fails.

Social Life

Another significant area of mental adjustment is your social life. God created human beings for fellowship with himself and with one another. However, you will find that differences in social likes and dislikes—that you never dreamed existed— will appear after marriage. One sports-enthusiast husband and his music-loving wife had this conversation about a year after they were married. He asked, "Why is it that you don't go to football games with me any more?" She replied, "Well, I really don't understand football and I just don't enjoy it." With exasperation he retorted, "I don't understand that. When we were going together you never turned me down when I invited you to go to a game and you always seemed to enjoy it." Her reply was enlightening. "Oh, that's easy to understand. I enjoyed being with you so much I didn't care where we went." She then asked, "Why is it that you don't take me to concerts any more the way you did when we were going together?" He replied, "I can't stand longhair music!"

Suddenly they both realized that in their courtship days their love for each other had anesthetized them to their social differences. The thrill and excitement of being together made unpleasant things enjoyable. This kind of enlightenment will appear to almost every couple in several areas of their social life after marriage. By facing their differences and "in honor preferring one another," this couple worked out a policy wherein the wife went with the husband to sporting events and the husband took the wife to some musicals. By patiently learning the significance of the third-down play, she began not only to understand football, but to become an avid fan. He in turn has gained a greater appreciation for classical music so that a concert is no longer "sheer torture" to him.

We are all subject to change, and many times our likes and dislikes are based purely on prejudice or bad experiences in the past. Being creatures of habit, we can cultivate new likes and dislikes by enthusiastically throwing ourselves into something for "love's sake."

Friends Are Important. Couples eventually seek the companionship of other couples. They soon find that his boyfriends and her girlfriends have differing interests and time schedules so that gradually, unless the friends also marry, they make a new set of friends and associates.

Friends have a great influence upon us, particularly as we socialize with them. It is most important, therefore, that Christians find some Christian friends as close companions. You will have other friends, too. Ask the Holy Spirit to help you introduce them to Christ. But you will need Christian friends to help you grow in faith.

The best place to find Christian companionship is in your church. Take an active part in the Sunday school and become involved in the couples' group of your age. Use your home to entertain other couples and be a friend to them. The old principle, "He that would have friends must show himself friendly," is also true for couples. One thing to bear in mind is that social life should not stop after marriage. Naturally, you will not have the whirlwind social life you experienced as a single person in your courting days, because now your money is being spent for more permanent things. Nevertheless, you need to relax together outside of the home occasionally. This area is another one in which adjustment can be made by communication and loving consideration.

Family
Your relationship to your partner's family is important. Occasionally a partner's parents will be so ideal that he never has problems with them, but frankly, that is an exception rather than the rule. Most parents find it difficult to clip all apron strings

after their children marry, even though they know they should. A couple should live separately from their parents, but be very respectful toward them. It is most natural for parents to offer advice based on their twenty or more years of experience, and sometimes couples rebel at this even to the point of rejecting good advice because it came from one of their parents.

Usually one's own parents are not as annoying as the partner's parents, simply because each one understands his own parents better. Many times an in-law's suggestions appear to be disapproval or judgment when in reality they were given with the best of intentions.

You can afford to be considerate and thoughtful of your partner's parents. After all, they spent many years and thousands of dollars preparing your mate. The least you can do is treat them with dignity and respect. Avoid speaking negatively to your partner's parents; if it is necessary to tell them they are interfering too much in your marriage, always let their offspring do the telling. It is probably wise that husband and wife go together, but the blood relative should state the situation.

The maternal instinct being what it is, mothers frequently have greater difficulty giving up their sons than do fathers their daughters. A loving wife should try to understand this and not put her husband into the difficult position of having to choose the one to whom he will be loyal, his wife or his mother. By thoughtfulness and love the wife can help the husband maintain a relaxed feeling toward his parents and particularly his mother. This considerateness will also benefit the wife. She can afford to be generous in this area. She has her husband now for much more time than his mother had him, and besides, she has a relationship to him that can never be shared by another woman, including his mother.

A husband should be very careful to avoid comparisons between his wife and his mother. It is entirely unfair to compare a young wife's ironing, cooking, and housekeeping abilities to those of a woman who has had twenty years of experience. Indulgence in unkind comparisons of this nature will only create hostilities and conflict between the two women most important to the husband.

Difficulties in family relationships should be talked over carefully and dealt with lovingly. It is possible, with God's help, to have an enjoyable relationship with in-laws that in turn enriches your marriage.

Appearance

Many a joke has been made about brides who come to the table with "stringy hair, sleepy eyes, and unpainted face" on the first morning after marriage. This moment of truth is no joking matter! Appearance isn't everything, but nevertheless it is important. The Bible tells us that "man looketh on the outward appearance, but the Lord looketh on the heart" (1 Samuel 16:7). Since your partner is human, he or she is going to look on your "outward appearance." It is therefore important that you do not use a wedding certificate as an excuse to relax your standards of appearance.

You would, no doubt, never have been attractive to your partner if you were not clean and neat in appearance. Help keep your partner's love alive by continuing to look well-groomed whenever possible. Your partner wants to be proud to introduce you to his or her friends; don't make your partner feel like apologizing for your appearance.

Men have a natural tendency to relax on their day off by not shaving. A look in the mirror will reveal that he scarcely looks his best in this unshaven condition. It is usually selfishness that causes a man not to shave on the day that he is with his wife the most—just because it is easier for him.

A bride should begin one ritual immediately after her honeymoon: the last thirty minutes before her husband returns from work she should spend on her appearance. His homecoming should be the high point in her day, and if she plans toward it she will always appear at first sight after his day's work the way she did when they were courting. This personal care is particularly needed in this day of men and women working together. A quick look in any office will reveal that working women try to look their best during the eight hours they are working with other women's husbands. If a wife lets her appearance run down, she puts herself in an unfavorable comparison to these women, and she may be just following the path of least resistance, which is a form of selfishness. Even after you have children, avoid using them as an excuse for shoddy or careless appearance—maintain your attractiveness to your companion.

Courtesy

Courtesy and manners are a grace that should become a part of every Christian's life, but in our modern civilization they seem to be a dying art. Courtesy is something taught a child by his parents and something a girl is able to demand of a boyfriend. The obvious time to discuss your differences on this matter is before marriage. Poor table manners and lack of normal courtesies can be a great source of irritation.

When my mother insisted that we always wear a shirt to the table, refrain from putting our elbows on the table, say please to one another, and use good manners in our treatment of each other, she remarked, "You will never be in better company than the company you are in right now." I am most grateful for her insistence upon these things, because I married a wife who enjoys courtesy and politeness—and I am inclined to believe that most women do.

A woman likes to be treated like a lady; therefore, a husband should be very careful not to stop giving his wife "preferential treatment" after they are married. It is a wise husband who opens doors, including car doors, for his wife and generally treats her as a gentleman should treat a lady. You will be making an investment in her happiness and self-respect, which will increase her love for you. Since love begets love, this is one of the best investments you can make in your marriage.

While holding a family conference in a church in Arizona, I announced one night that the next

17

evening I would tell men "how to get your wife to treat you like a king." For some strange reason we had our largest crowd that night. My advice startled some of the men by its simplicity, for I said: "Treat her like a queen!"

One almost inexcusable practice in marriage is disloyalty. Have you ever been out socially and heard a wife or husband berate and criticize the partner in front of mutual friends? This embarrassing practice is engaged in by partners who do not seem to be able to communicate in private and seek the safety of the group to vent their pent-up wrath. It is one of the most damaging wrongs a person can use against his or her partner.

Never, *never* air your partner's shortcomings, weaknesses, or deficiencies in front of other people. Never criticize him to your friends or relatives. If you are displeased with your partner's behavior on a matter, there are only two with whom you should share it: God and your partner. "But I have to have someone I can tell my problems to" is the usual defensive retort. As a Christian you have someone to whom you can take your problems: your heavenly Father. Then through prayer and the leading of the Holy Spirit, share the problems with your partner. If this does not work, talk the matter over with your pastor or counselor.

A lovely Christian mother whose daughter married one of the finest young men in our church came to see me one day. She was troubled over her feeling of animosity and bitterness toward her son-in-law and was finding it increasingly difficult to be nice to him. After talking to her and her daughter I found the cause. Two weeks after the couple returned from their honeymoon they had a fight. The daughter called her mother and told her the whole story. That night the husband came home and apologized for his short-tempered treatment of his bride, and they had one of those wonderful "making up" experiences that is such a uniting blessing in marriage.

A few weeks later another argument occurred, and she called her mother during the day to pour out her troubled heart. Without realizing it she called her mother only to tell about the problems they had; she had not called her back to tell about the tender moments of "making up." Consequently, after a few months the mother had only one side of the story of their relationship. It was no wonder that she thought of her new son-in-law as an "ill-tempered brute." By sharing the joys of her marriage with her mother thereafter, the daughter put an end to her mother's resentment toward the son-in-law.

You should never criticize your partner to others for two reasons. First, rehearsing grudges or nursing gripes stamps them more indelibly upon your mind. Second, the desire for approval is one of the basic drives of man. Nothing can make a person feel less approved of than to find that his partner has been so disloyal as to criticize him to an outsider. If needed, your pastor or a professional counselor can be consulted, but don't discuss the situation with anyone else.

Be Open to Change

Most spontaneous decisions or prejudices are the result of our background, but that does not determine whether they are right or wrong. I have met men who—because their father did not treat their mother that way—refuse to give in to their wife's desire that they be more gentlemanly and polite. Actually, that reason has nothing to do with it. Just because a man's father made a lifetime of mistakes is no reason his son should perpetuate them. Therefore, whenever you go into a communication session with your partner regarding the mental adjustments of your marriage, always bear in mind that the standards and concepts produced by your background could be wrong. There may be another way of doing it. Remember, one of the characteristics of love is "love seeketh not her own . . ." (1 Corinthians 13:5).

Adjusting in marriage can be a thrilling experience through which you can improve yourself by embracing the strengths of your partner's background and temperament. Be willing to bend and give. Don't resist change in your behavior unless it is behavior for which the Scripture has already set a standard. Be objective about the differences between you and your partner, because just as you expect him to change in some areas, he has a right to expect change from you. Fortunately, change is a natural part of life. One of the happy observations I have made is that many of our "likes" today were "hates" ten years ago. Give your partner time to adjust, and you will find that time draws two unselfish people together.

THE KEYS

Many a time I have wished I were a magician! When a married couple tells me their problems and resultant miseries, I would love to wave a magic wand over them and watch them leave my office to "live happily ever after."

Naturally, I don't have such a wand. But I do have six keys that are guaranteed to open the door to a happy marriage. Examine each key carefully. The degree to which you use them determines the success of your marriage. If you neglect them, your marriage cannot help but be a miserable and wretched experience. These keys come from the Bible, God's manual on human behavior. Therefore, I can guarantee happiness and success to all who use them.

Key of Maturity

The first key that guarantees happiness in marriage is *maturity*. This key is best expressed in the emotional realm as unselfishness. Babies and small children are selfish—thus we refer to them as immature. When a child throws a fit in a supermarket by lying on the floor and screaming, because he can't have his way, he is revealing his selfishness or immaturity.

If such a child is not properly disciplined, he will go into marriage so immature that he will want his own way in practically every situation. Such an attitude, very subtle and difficult for the immature person to recognize, is disastrous to a marriage.

The Problem. The adjustment stage of marriage, usually considered the first three years, will naturally produce conflicts of interest. For the first twenty or more years of their lives, people function as independent gears. They make decisions purely on the basis of what they want or what is good for them. After the wedding, two independent individuals must learn to mesh together. Since they are both moving objects, and all movement creates friction, there is bound to be friction as they learn to move together in unity.

Marriage consists of a series of actions and reactions motivated by our conscious and subconscious minds. The more active the people, the more potential areas of conflict can be expected. Conflict, however, need not be fatal. In fact, some counselors suggest that conflicts are normal and can provide a creative force in marriage. Dr. Alfred B. Messer, addressing the American Psychiatric Convention in October of 1966, said, "A spirited spat is good for most marriages.... Arguments are inevitable in a marriage and probably offer one of the best ways couples have to work out touchy problems. When most of the frustrations have been

22

talked out or discharged in some vicarious way, the fight can be ended. Those marriages that exist without any type of fighting are generally frozen or inflexible marriages in which other aspects of the relationship are compromised in order to maintain the facade of peace and harmony."

Although some conflict is inevitable between two normal human beings, fighting is not the answer. By God's grace, two mature people can face their areas of conflict, discuss them, and by obeying the injunctions of God's Word resolve them. Don't get into the habit of sweeping your problems under the rug. Face them and resolve them in the Spirit. Actually, there is nothing wrong with having a conflict of interest between husband and wife. In fact, every such case is a test of your maturity. The partner that demands "his own way" in such conflicts is traveling a collision course that will produce much unhappiness for both of them.

You Never Get by Getting. After I completed a marriage counseling session some years ago, the prospective bride looked at me and said, "Your advice is sure different from the advice the girls at the office gave me. They said, 'Bonnie, one thing to remember in marriage is that men are out for all they can get. Don't give too much of yourself to your husband; he'll just take advantage of you.' " That unchristian and unsound attitude is one of the things that produces so much misery in homes.

In God's economy, you never get anything by getting; the way to have something is to give it away. If you want love, for example, don't look for it—give it. If you want friends, don't look for friends—be friendly. The same is true of thoughtfulness, consideration, and selflessness. If you want your partner to treat you unselfishly, then be mature enough by God's grace to treat him or her unselfishly.

Why did you get married in the first place? The answer to that question may give you an insight into your maturity. Did you get married because "I had an unhappy home life" or because "I got tired of my parents' telling me what to do" or because "All of my friends were getting married and I didn't want to be left alone" or because "I wanted somebody to love me"? The proper attitude that guarantees success in a marriage is based on mature unselfishness. Mature individuals will go into marriage not only for what they can get out of it, but for what they can give to their partners. Two verses in the Bible come close to being a "magic wand"; when used by marriage partners, they turn chaos into peace and harmony:

"Let nothing be done through strife or vainglory; but in lowliness of mind let each esteem other better than themselves. Look not every man on his own things, but every man also on the things of others" (Philippians 2:3-4).

If you go into marriage with this attitude—"look not on your own things... but on the things of your partner"—you will discover happiness in your home. Your attitude should never be that it is your partner's responsibility to make you happy. You

24

must initially recognize your responsibility to make your partner happy.

There is an irrelevant and erroneous saying about marriage that has somehow become popular: "Marriage is a fifty-fifty proposition." Nothing could be further from the truth! Marriage, under God, should be a one hundred percent-to-nothing proposition. That is, you should go into your marriage with the idea that you are going to give yourself one hundred percent for the purpose of making your partner happy and expect nothing in return. The result will be your own happiness.

A sharp young couple came to see me some years ago with conflict written all over their marriage. George had come from a very secure home. His greatest pleasure was to go hunting with his father on weekends. Ellen came from a very insecure home where her parents' many conflicts produced an early desire in her to get married and get away from it all. After four years of marriage they had discovered that although their love was not yet destroyed, they were at such cross purposes that they knew it soon would be if something were not done.

I soon discovered that they had entirely different concepts of married life. Ellen, who was inclined to escape the nasty realities of *now* by dreaming about an Utopian future, wanted marriage to be a "blissful time of relaxation and family life, particularly on weekends." George thought marriage should be a relaxed home life five nights a week, with most weekends spent hunting and fishing with his father and some day, he hoped, with his son. In fact, he wanted to get married as soon as he did because he spent so much time with Ellen while courting her that he had to give up some of his treasured hunting experiences.

Strangely enough, they both knew what the problem was; they just had never faced it before. Every time he planned a trip with his father, Ellen would become angry and they would exchange cutting remarks. When she crawled into her self-protective shell of silence and frigidity, it was even worse. Sometimes he couldn't enjoy the hunting trip because he knew things were not right at home.

Fortunately, these two people were mature enough to face the fact that their marriage was more important than "togetherness" or hunting trips. We worked out an agreement in which they would both give in to the other's desires on this matter. George went on only half as many hunting trips and Ellen tried hard to send him out of town in a good spirit. Several times she didn't feel very good about it, but for his sake she tried vigorously and succeeded.

Then one day a friend invited them to go water skiing. Both were excellent swimmers, and they took to this form of entertainment like ducks to water. A few weeks later they bought a boat and now regularly go out on Saturdays with friends for an enjoyable time together.

Was it a great sacrifice for George? When I asked him some months later how things were going, he replied, "For some reason I've lost a lot of my interest in hunting and fishing. I only go three or four times a year now. I would rather go water skiing with Ellen, or do something else with her and the children." Don't be afraid of giving in; you win in the long run.

Selfishness Is Universal. Selfishness, the greatest single enemy to a happy marriage, is a part of man's basic nature. All temperaments have the weakness of selfishness in common, though it is revealed differently. The strong extrovert reveals his selfishness in egotism and angry impatience toward others; the moderate extrovert exhibits his selfishness in angry and cruel disregard for the feelings of others. The sensitive introvert displays his selfishness through introspection that produces fear and indecision. The quiet and easygoing temperament shows stubborn refusal to get involved with the problems of others lest he be hurt.[2]

The important thing to remember is that something can be done to overcome selfishness. The Bible tells us in 2 Corinthians 5:17, "Therefore if any man be in Christ, he is a new creature: old things are passed away; behold, all things are become new." The Greek construction of this verse indicates the gradual passing away of old things, which includes man's natural selfishness. When Jesus Christ comes to live in a person's life, he creates a new nature within him that, if yielded to and nurtured, will overpower the old nature.

How to Overcome Selfishness. Selfishness can be corrected by the power of God in conjunction with

[2]*Spirit-Controlled Temperament,* Tim LaHaye, Tyndale House.

27

a cooperative individual. God will give you the power if you are willing to cooperate with him. The following steps are highly successful in changing selfish behavior into unselfish acts of thoughtfulness toward others.

1. Face your selfishness as a sin! Until you are able to recognize your selfishness as a sin displeasing to God and to others, you will never be able to think of others before you think of yourself. Too many people excuse it on the basis that "I was given a free hand by my parents and I just developed the habit of doing whatever I want." The fact that your parents made the mistake of indulging you by not limiting your activities to those areas that were good for you is no reason to perpetuate that mistake for a lifetime. Instead, face it as a sin.

2. Don't try to hide behind academic or economic success to cover your selfishness. Maturity is relative. That is, a man may be a brilliant scientist and a good leader at work, but a selfish, overgrown baby as a husband at home. A woman may be an effective organizer and women's club president or church worker, but a selfish, childish, miserable wife. Face the truth that no matter what you are in the business or academic world, if you fail in your marriage, you have failed in an important area of your life. Selfishness is the greatest cause of marital failure.

Once you have faced the fact that your selfishness, regardless of your partner's behavior, is a sin before God, you have made a giant step. Before you will submit to an operation, your doctor must convince you that you have a disease or some other physical malady. Excusing the symptoms will never correct the problem. The same principle applies in the emotional realm. As long as you cover up your selfishness, excuse it, or ignore it, you will never correct it. Happy is the man who understands that he, and he alone before God, is responsible for his actions and reactions, and that when he acts with a selfish motive he has sinned against God as well as against his fellow man.

3. Confess your selfishness as a sin. There are no big sins or little sins in God's sight. Sin is sin. Whenever you act selfishly, be sufficiently objective about yourself to confess your sin to your heavenly Father, then be assured that he will forgive you (1 John 1:9).

4. Ask God to take away the habit of being selfish. "And this is the confidence that we have in him, that, if we ask any thing according to his will, he heareth us: And if we know that he hears us, whatsoever we ask, we know that we have the petitions that we desired of him" (1 John 5:14, 15). Since it is not God's will that we be selfish creatures, he will direct us in changing our habit of behaving selfishly.

5. Repair the damage done by your selfishness. Whether or not he deserves it, apologize to the one to whom you exhibited your immaturity or self-seeking and you will find it easier and easier to avoid selfish behavior. A person soon learns that he would rather not be selfish because it is harder to humble himself enough to say, "I was wrong. Will you forgive me?" than to give up selfish behavior!

6. Repeat this formula every time you do or say something under the motivation of selfishness. It will help you become a happy, well-adjusted, and unselfish person whose company other people enjoy. In addition, your maturity may gradually inspire maturity in your partner. Before you realize it, the key of maturity will open many doors to happiness in your marriage.

Key of Submission

No organization can function properly if it has two heads. That is particularly true of the home. One of the great hindrances to a happy home today is the false notion that a woman does not have to subject herself to her husband. Modern psychology and education seem to give women the idea that subjection is an old-fashioned notion that went out with the nineteenth century. But when subjection goes out of the home, so does happiness. *Wifely submission* is the second key.

Today we have more frustrated women, men, and children than ever before. With the downgrading of the father image and the rising dominance of the mother role, we have witnessed an increase in juvenile delinquency, rebellion, homosexuality, and divorce. God intended man to be the head of his home. If he is not, he will not have a sense of responsibility but will subconsciously feel he is married to a second mother. His children will soon detect who is boss, and as teen-agers they will lose the natural respect for their father that is necessary for their adjustment to life.

30

Usually a wife-dominated home is a quarrelsome home until the husband finally "gives up." He then crawls into his shell of introversion and degenerates into a sub-par human being. The sadder result is, a wife will eventually grow to despise the husband she dominates.

A Command of God. The Christian woman must be in subjection to her husband! Whether she likes it or not, subjection is a command of God and her refusal to comply with this command is an act of disobedience. All disobedience is sin; therefore, she cannot expect the blessing of God on her life unless she is willing to obey God. The following Scripture passages establish this fact.

"Unto the woman he said, I will greatly multiply thy sorrow and thy conception; in sorrow thou shalt bring forth children; and thy desire shall be to thy husband, and he shall rule over thee" (Genesis 3:16). "Wives, submit yourselves unto your own husbands, as unto the Lord. For the husband is the head of the wife, even as Christ is the head of the church: and he is the savior of the body. Therefore as the church is subject unto Christ, so let the wives be to their own husbands in every thing . . . and the wife see that she reverence her husband" (Ephesians 5:22-24, 33).

"Likewise, ye wives, be in subjection to your own husbands; that, if any obey not the Word, they also may without the Word be won by the conversation of the wives; while they behold your chaste conversation coupled with fear" (1 Peter 3:1-2).

The refusal of many Christian wives to accept the principle of subjection is increasingly common today. A number of years ago I taught a Bible class of forty-five adults—twenty-three women and twenty-two men. I described the results of the curse of Genesis 3 on the man, the woman, and the ground and the serpent. Concerning the woman, I pointed out that she had two parts to her curse: one, sorrow in childbirth; two, being ruled over by her husband. The next week I gave an examination and believe it or not, in response to the question, "What was the result of the curse to the woman?" I received twenty-three female answers: "She shall have sorrow in childbirth" and the twenty-two men answered, "She shall be ruled over by her husband." A few of the men also included that she would have sorrow in childbirth. The fact that not one of those twenty-three women, who voluntarily attended that Bible class for the purpose of spiritual growth, had remembered the subjection part of the curse illustrated to me the universal tendency of women to reject this God-given command.

God's Tool for Your Happiness. God never commands people to do that which is impossible or is not for their good. The Holy Spirit has asked in Romans 8:32, "He that spared not his own Son, but delivered him up for us all, how shall he not with him also freely give us all things?" The answer to that is, if God loved us so much that he gave his Son to die for us, certainly he will give us all those things that are for our good. Therefore, accept the fact by faith that submission to her husband is for a woman's good.

Somewhere between thirty-five and forty-five a woman usually reaches a period when she increasingly desires to become a leaner. If she is aggressive in the early years of marriage and dominates her husband, she teaches him to lean on her. Then when she gets to the age where she wants a man to lean on, she finds that she has created a leaner and has no one on whom she *can* lean. I've seen many a woman at this stage come to loathe the man whom she in her younger years trained to be a docile, submissive spouse.

It is an act of faith in a Christian woman's heart to assume that for her lasting happiness and the happiness of her husband it is essential that she be obedient to God and put herself in subjection to her husband.

Subjection Is Not Slavery. When a Christian woman seeks God's grace and the filling of the Holy Spirit to enable her to live in subjection to her husband, she is not in danger of becoming a slave. Many times I have seen women subject themselves for spiritual reasons and find that the reaction in their husband has been one of thoughtfulness and kindness which caused a cessation of hostilities between them. Usually a woman finds that she fares far better when she is in subjection than when she dominates. Certainly she will enjoy a better walk with God when she is obedient to her husband for the Lord's sake, than when she disobeys God by dominating her husband.

Subjection does not mean that a woman can't voice her opinion by "speaking the truth in love" (Ephesians 4:15), but that she should seek to be

33

submissive to her husband's desires when he reaches a decision, and that she comply with his requirements whenever possible. There may be times when she will have to do something that she really doesn't want to do, but by sowing the seeds of obedience on that matter she will reap the harvest of blessing on many others. Always remember, you reap far more than you sow. If you sow submission in obedience to God, you will reap blessing in abundance; if you sow rebellion in disobedience to the will of God, you will reap abundant misery. Some women have a more aggressive temperament than their husbands and admittedly it is more difficult for them to be in subjection. In fact, the only way I know they can is to recognize that it is a spiritual responsibility. When this fact has been established in her mind, any woman can summon the grace of God to be the submissive person God wants her to be.

Some years ago I counseled with a woman who was far more aggressive than her husband and found that through the years she had made the major decisions of the family even though he was well-educated. He was an easygoing phlegmatic person and she was a combination of sanguine and choleric temperament. Thus, when children came in to ask questions he would be relaxed and quiet while she answered and made decisions. At about thirty-five years of age she recognized that he was gradually receding into a shell of compliance in the home and she was assuming dictatorial powers. When she became convinced of her need to submit to her husband for the Lord's sake, she asked God to help her

34

bite her tongue and stifle her intuitive inclination to make spontaneous decisions—and to wait for her husband to make the decision. She was amazed to find that in a brief period of time he rose to the challenge and gradually assumed the decision-making prerogatives in the home. Interesting to me as I counseled with this woman was the fact that the more she submitted, the more he led; the more he led, the happier he was; and the happier he was, the happier she was. That marriage was gradually changed from the level of staying together because they were Christians to a new height of genuine love and respect for each other. To me, this couple is a living example of the fact that a wife's submission to her husband is a key to a happy marriage.

Key of Love

The third key that guarantees a happy marriage is *love*. Probably no other word in the English language is more misunderstood than this one. Most people today do not know what love is. They often confuse physical attraction, lust, personal desire, sympathy, or compassion with love. Love is one of the most common experiences of man and one of the most difficult to define. Webster defines it as "a feeling of strong personal attachment induced by sympathetic understanding, or by ties of kinship; ardent affection."

The Bible says the love of a husband for his wife should equal his love for himself. God instructed him to love his wife sacrificially as Christ loved the

Church and gave himself for her (the Church). No woman can be unhappy when given that kind of love, and the husband who gives that kind of love will be the recipient of sacrificial love.

Like God, love cannot be seen, but we know of its existence because of its effects. It is easier to describe love than define it. Although many have attempted a description of love, in all the annals of literature there is none that compares with those masterful words that come from the pen of the Apostle Paul in the great love chapter, 1 Corinthians 13. Note this beautiful description as it appears in *The Living Bible* paraphrase by Kenneth Taylor (verses 4-7):

"Love is very patient and kind, never jealous or envious, never boastful or proud, never haughty or selfish or rude. Love does not demand its own way. It is not irritable or touchy. It does not hold grudges and will hardly even notice when others do it wrong. It is never glad about injustice, but rejoices whenever truth wins out. If you love someone, you will be loyal to him no matter what the cost. You will always believe in him, always expect the best of him, and always stand your ground in defending him."

Henry Drummond, in a book titled *The Greatest Thing in the World*, points out the nine characteristics of love found in this preceding passage: patience, kindness, generosity, humility, courtesy, unselfishness, good temper, guilelessness, and sincerity. Study these characteristics and examine your love to see if it meets God's standards of acceptable expression.

These nine characteristics or expressions of love communicate the love of one human being to another in terms that are meaningful to everyone, regardless of race or background. No one will naturally express his love in all of these characteristics. Some people are patient and kind by nature, but lack humility, generosity, or confidence. Others are naturally sincere and courteous, but lack a good temper and are prone to be impatient. All men need the power of the Holy Spirit to supply the kind of love God expects us to extend to our partner. The Holy Spirit gives Christians the ability to express complete love (Galatians 5:22, 23).

The love that God requires of a husband for his wife and the wife for her husband is admittedly a supernatural love. Self-preservation is the first law of life; therefore, to love someone else as your own body demands a supernatural kind of love. It is just not possible for man to love this way of his own accord. However, since God never commands us to do that which he will not enable us to do, we can call upon him, the author of love, and know that he will supply us with that kind of supernatural love. The Bible tells us, "Beloved, let us love one another, for love is of God, and every one that loveth is born of God and knoweth God" (1 John 4:7).

Both husband and wife are commanded to love each other, but it should be pointed out that while the wife is commanded once (Titus 2:4) to love her husband, the husband is commanded at least three times to love his wife (Ephesians 5:25, 28, 33). The reason is probably that women by nature are more inclined to demonstrate love.

Love Is Kind. One of the primary characteristics of love is kindness. Somehow, many of the couples having trouble in marriage have forgotten to show kindness. They want to receive it, but they forget to give it. A couple who had been married two years came to see me, fulfilling the promise I require of all young couples before marriage that they will not separate from each other before they come and talk the matter over with me. They were ready to call it quits even though they had a little love left in their marriage. The problem was they were very caustic, sarcastic, and cutting in their speech toward each other. When this was revealed in counseling, I gave them the assignment of memorizing the nine characteristics of love and, since kindness to each other was conspicuously absent, I asked them to give their conversation "the kindness check." That is, every time they said something to each other they were to ask themselves, "Was that kind?" If it was not, they were to apologize and seek God's grace to be kind. Obviously, it was difficult for a time, but within two months this couple had reoriented themselves to the point that they could be kind to each other and the result was a renewing of their genuine affection for each other.

Love Shows Approval. Most psychologists agree that the basic needs of man are love and approval. The more we love someone, the more we naturally seek his approval. For that reason, if a person does not express his love by showing approval occasionally, he will have a dissatisfied mate.

A couple came to see me one time that were complete opposites physically. The man was six-feet-four and weighed at least 235 pounds—a real football type. The woman could not have weighed over 105 pounds and was probably about five feet tall. In the course of counseling, he said in an emotion-packed voice, "Pastor I haven't hit that woman in all the years we have been married," and as he said it he doubled up his gigantic fist. I looked at her, and saw tears running down her cheeks as she dejectedly said, "That's true, but many times I wish he would hit me instead of everlastingly clubbing me with disapproval!"

I honestly believe that disapproval is a more vicious way of inflicting punishment upon another human being than physical abuse. And the sad part is, the thing people disapprove of in their partner is usually blown up out of proportion, making the problem greater than it is. Many a man would have to admit that he has a good wife, and the thing that aggravates him comprises only ten to fifteen percent of the total person. His problem is that he has concentrated too much on the negative instead of thanking God for the positive. It is good to frequently ask yourself, "Do I express approval of my partner?" That approval should be expressed both publicly, to assure your friends that you love your partner, and privately. Many a man has been given a neater house by commending his wife for those areas that are neat rather than condemning her for those that are messy. Be sure of one thing, your partner needs your approval for his or her adjustment in life and marriage. Most people respond better to commendation than to condemnation.

Love Can Be Rekindled. "I just don't love my husband any more!" said a young woman whose husband was not a Christian. She was looking for the wrong way to escape—divorce. Not loving your partner does not necessarily testify to the unloveliness of the partner, but it does reveal your own lack of love. God will give you love for your partner if you seek it! As we have already seen, love is of God (1 John 4:7). If you want to love your partner, you can! God has commanded you to love him, or her, and he will enable you to if you ask him. In fact, the first characteristic of the Spirit-filled life is "love" (Galatians 5:22). If you find your love beginning to wane, then go to your heavenly Father, the author of love, and he will give you a new love for your partner. It is yours for the asking! You may be inclined to ask, "But is it worth it?" or "What if my partner doesn't deserve it?" That has nothing to do with it. You should love your partner for the Lord's sake; but, because of the principle of reaping what you sow, loving will bring you love. If you go to God by faith for his supply of love to give to your partner, then God's divine law will bring love to you.

The young woman previously mentioned prayed for that kind of love, and God gave it. Then after a church service she said to me, "You just wouldn't believe the way God has restored my love for my husband! In fact, he has never been more loving and considerate in the eight years we have been married."

Women Respond to Love. I never cease to marvel at the endurance of a woman's love. Women have told me things about their husbands that could earn them the title, "the meanest man in town," yet these women end up by saying, "but I still love him." Men would never put up with some of the things that women are forced to endure. It must be a carryover of a mother's love, which we tend to think of as the greatest illustration of human love. Whatever the cause, I am convinced that a woman has a far greater capacity to love a man than a man has to love a woman. I have yet to see a woman who will not respond to love.

No man in his right mind would present himself as an authority on women. Most of us say they are complex creatures, and they are. Like other men I do not claim to be an authority on feminine matters, but after counseling several hundred of the so-called "weaker sex" I have come to one basic conclusion. Most American men do not know how to make a woman happy. I have learned that it isn't money, diamonds, furs, houses, or other things that make a woman happy, but just plain love. Not love-making, but the treatment that produces love-making—kindness, thoughtfulness, understanding, acceptance or approval, and the recognition by the husband that he is just not complete without her. Happy is the wife whose husband knows and tells her that he would choose the same bride if given the chance to marry all over again. *Whenever*

41

a man tells me, "My wife doesn't love me anymore,"
I immediately know that he is a man who has not loved
his wife "as his own body." If he had, she would
return his love—that's just the nature of women.

Key of Communication

Young lovers rarely have a communication problem! Somehow, that ability often vanishes after
they are married. *Communication* is the third key
to a happy home.

Lack of communication is almost always a problem for the couples who come to me for marriage
counseling. If it is not lack of communication, it
is wrong communication. Communicating under
pressure of anger and shouting at the top of one's
voice is the wrong approach. This is communication that could well be omitted in every marriage.
*Problems and differences in a marriage are not dan-
gerous—not being able to communicate the differences,*
or problem areas, is dangerous. As long as two people
can keep the lines of communication open and
freely express their feelings, differences can be
resolved.

The following statement by Ann Landers in her
syndicated column illustrates the importance of
communication. "The most important single ingre-
dient in a marriage is the ability to communicate.
If my mail is a fair reflection of what goes on with
Mr. and Mrs. America behind closed doors (and I
think it is), most marital problems stem from the
inability of two people to talk to each other. How
precious is the ability to communicate! . . . The

42

mature man and woman recognize that there is unity in love, but at the same time there must be freedom for both individuals. Neither should be swallowed up by the other. Each must maintain his personality and his identity. A sound marriage should mean togetherness, but it also should mean respect for the rights and privileges of the other party. The couples who are secure in marriage can be honest about all kinds of feelings. . . . The man and wife who can air their differences, get the hostility out of their system, then kiss and make up have an excellent chance of growing old together."

It has been amazing to me to find that many couples settle for a second-rate marriage relationship primarily because they have never learned to communicate. A few years ago a woman who did not know I had already talked with her husband came to me for counseling. Their problem seemed to be that the woman was not completely committed to the Lord. But her lack of commitment to Christ was not the real problem. A few weeks later she gave me a ride home after a meeting and spontaneously invited me in to talk to both of them. Her husband was surprised, but quickly responded; and suddenly I was acting as a referee between two friends. For twenty minutes she calmly mentioned some of her pet gripes and objections to her husband. None of them was unusual or severe, but added together they created a spirit of resentment in her. Some things went back to within six months after they were married. When she finished, he very calmly said to her, "Honey, why in the world didn't you tell me these things years ago?" (They had been married ten years.) Her answer was, "I was afraid to. I thought you would explode."

Knowing that every argument has two sides, I asked the husband if he would like to voice his objections to her as kindly as he could. For a similar period of time he then rehearsed her weaknesses and when he finished, she turned and said, "Why didn't you tell me this before?" He replied, "Because I thought you would get mad and go into a long period of silence." By learning to communicate, that couple soon learned to exchange their honest feelings without fear and the wife was able to fully commit herself to Christ.

Communication Killers. How does the wall of resistance to communication gradually build up between two people who love each other? Naturally, neither plans the erection of such a wall; it gradually grows from the time of their first breakdown in communication. Psychologist Dr. Henry Brandt shared with a group of ministers the three weapons that people use to defend themselves. As you look at these three weapons, you see that they gradually build a wall of resistance to communication.

The first weapon is *explosion*. Whenever a person is told his shortcomings, his natural reaction is to explode rather than face them honestly. This explosion is the result of inner anger and hostility that causes him to attempt self-protection. Dr. Brandt points out that no nakedness is comparable to psychological nakedness. When someone, particularly our partner, points out our deficiencies

44

we tend to grasp for something to cover us; and if we happen to be sanguine or choleric in temperament we will tend to use anger and express it through explosion. This teaches our partner that: "You can't come that close to my weaknesses; if you do, I'll explode."

The second self-defense weapon that hinders communication is *tears*. This weapon is used mostly by women, though sometimes a melancholy or sanguine man will resort to it. Like the other weapons, it is a way of saying to your partner, "Don't tell me my shortcomings or I'll cry!" The first spat after marriage often leaves the bride in tears. This teaches the new husband that she has a breaking point and subconsciously he will thereafter tend to hold back his communication lest he make her cry. Thus, another block is laid in the wall that impedes communication.

A parenthetical note is appropriate here on feminine tears. Husband, learn to distinguish between your wife's tears of emotion, stress, joy, and self-pity. Women are far more intricate creatures than men, and often show their emotions through tears. Don't despise your wife's tears! Be patient and kind, for the emotional creature you married is just being a woman. In fact, I have found that the woman who is easily moved to tears has the greatest capacity to express her emotions in every area of life. Usually that type of wife is more responsive to tenderness and lovemaking than the dry-eyed girl. In fact, women who weep easily are seldom frigid, and tearless wives often have emotions like an iceberg. I have counseled more than one thousand women and have had no reason to change this conclusion. If your wife is emotionally expressive, thank God! Her tears testify to this emotional richness that makes her a compassionate mother and loving wife. Be particularly thoughtful during her menstrual period, as she may be unusually emotional then. "Tender loving care" during that period is like laying up treasure in heaven—it pays off by and by.

The third weapon is *silence*. Silence is the weapon that many older Christians learn to use. It is not long before we realize that it isn't Christian to get mad and explode all over the neighborhood when our partner crosses us or points out our weaknesses. Then, too, as children come along we are reluctant to weep in front of them; therefore, Christians resort to silence. Silence, however, is a very dangerous tool. It is dangerous in that it eliminates communication and takes a heavy toll physically and spiritually upon a person. It takes tremendous power to be silent for a long period of time, power that is fueled by deepening anger. Since anger is one of the leading causes of ulcers, high blood pressure, and many other diseases, you will find that silence is a very expensive tool to use.

Some years ago I counseled with a couple, and one of their problems was that the man was very slow of speech and his wife was just the opposite. Whenever he would try to express himself, she would give the rebuttal to his statement even before he had finished. Her constant chatter reminded me of a machine gun as she blasted away at him. He soon learned that he was no match for her in an argument. One day I met him at church and just casually asked, "How are things going?" "Wonderful," he said. "I finally found out how to handle that woman!"

When I asked him how he did it, he said, "Through silence. The one thing she can't stand is for me to be silent. When she crosses me I will go for long periods without talking. In fact, I even went five days one time without speaking to her." My answer to him was, "That is going to be a very expensive tool because pent-up anger and bitterness produce ulcers." Little did I realize how prophetic my statement was for in a matter of weeks I got the report that he had a bleeding ulcer.

How much better it would be if two people would learn to freely communicate their differences, and thereby avoid not only problems but also the side effects. Remember, all anger, bitterness, and wrath grieve the Holy Spirit (Ephesians 4:30-32). No man can "walk in the Spirit" and be mad at his wife (Galatians 5:16).

How to Communicate. The Bible teaches that we should "speak the truth in love . . ." (Ephesians 4:15). One should bear in mind, however, that the more truth you would speak, the more love you should use in conveying that truth. Truth is a sharp, two-edged sword, so use it carefully. When you have an area in your marriage that needs communication, consider using the following steps in presenting your case.

1. Pray for the wisdom of God and the filling of the Holy Spirit. When you seek God's wisdom you

may find that your objection to your partner's behavior is not really valid. Or you may sense the leading of the Spirit of God to go ahead and communicate your problem.

2. Plan a time that is good for your partner. Usually you should not discuss anything of a serious or negative nature after 10 or 10:30 P.M. Life tends to look darker and problems loom greater at night. However, if your partner is not an early riser, the morning is not the best time either. Many couples find a good time for communication is after supper. Small children can often make this less than desirable, but each couple should find a time when they are in the best possible mood to look objectively at themselves.

3. Speak the truth in love—in kind words say exactly what is on your heart. Make sure that your love is equal to your truth.

4. Don't lose your temper. Wise couples determine early in their marriage that they will not raise their voices at each other. Under anger we often say more than we intend and usually this excess is cutting, cruel, and unnecessary. Anger on one person's part usually precipitates an angry response by the other. Kindly state your objection in love and only once, then trust the Holy Spirit to use your words in effecting a change.

5. Allow for reaction time. Don't be surprised if your communication is met with an explosive reaction, particularly in the earlier stages of marriage. Remember, you have the advantage in that you know what you are going to say; you have prayed it over and have been able to prepare your-

self—your partner is taken by surprise. Don't defend yourself, but let your partner think about what you have said. He or she may never admit that you are right, but often you will find that it will create a change in his behavior and, after all, you are more interested in that than you are in verbal agreement.

6. Commit the problem to God. Once you have told your partner, you have done about all you can do, humanly speaking, to change his behavior. From that point on you must trust God either to help your partner change his objectionable habit or to supply you with the necessary grace to live with it (2 Corinthians 12:9).

Two Golden Expressions. There are two golden expressions that every married couple should communicate to their partner repeatedly throughout their marriage.

"I'm sorry." Everyone makes mistakes. Romans 3:23 points out that "all have sinned, and come short of the glory of God." You will sin against your partner, and your partner will sin against you many times in a normal marriage. If, however, you are willing to face your mistakes and apologize to your companion, you will find that resistance will dissolve and a spirit of forgiveness will prevail. If you are unwilling to acknowledge your mistakes, then you have a serious spiritual problem—pride.

One time I counseled with a couple and the wife tearfully said, "My husband has never apologized to me in the twenty-three years we have been married." Turning to him, I asked him if he had ever done anything wrong. He quickly replied,

"Oh, of course, I am only human." I then asked, "Why have you never apologized?" His reply was, "I didn't think it was manly for me to apologize; my father never apologized to my mother." Unfortunately, this man grew up under a father who made a terrible decision never to apologize. Now this man was perpetuating that mistake and reaping the resultant misery. When you are wrong, face it objectively and honestly admit it—both to yourself and to your partner.

"I love you" is the second golden expression in a marriage. I have already pointed out that it is absolutely necessary for every human being to be loved. Your partner will never tire of hearing you tell him or her of your love. This expression of love seems to be more meaningful to women than men, but I am inclined to believe women are just more prone to admit the need for it, and that men need it also.

A man came to see me the day after his wife of fifteen years had left him. He was an engineer with an I.Q. of 148, he said, and made "$15,000 a year." As he told me about the shipwreck of his marriage, he acknowledged that for ten years he had not told his wife he loved her. When I asked him why, he said, "Why should I have to tell her? I have demonstrated it faithfully for fifteen years. She didn't like the house we lived in, so I bought her another house. She didn't like her car, so I bought her another car to run around in. She didn't like the carpeting, so I had it taken out and new carpeting put in. If I didn't love her, would I have given her five children?"

The amazing thing about the whole affair was

that his wife had run off with a sailor who made $275 a month and looked enough like her husband to be his twin brother. In exasperation he said to me, "What could that poor sailor possibly give to my wife that I haven't already given her?" My answer was, "Just one thing, love."

As brilliant a scientist as he was, this man was an ignoramus as a husband. Their problem could have been solved if he had been willing to give of himself and let her know that he loved her and approved of her. He couldn't seem to understand that although saying "I love you" sounded childish to him, it was meaningful to her. Nor did he understand that if he had not been so selfish he would have been more than willing to express in words what she wanted to hear. The more your partner loves you, the more he enjoys hearing you express your love. Say it meaningfully and say it often.

Key of Prayer

The keys to a happy marriage would not be complete if I did not include *prayer*. Prayer to their heavenly Father is the best means of communication between two people. *Many a marriage has been completely transformed by initiating a time of regular prayer.* One method I heartily recommend is conversational prayer. I learned about this method from a magazine article about the prayer life of Dr. and Mrs. Ralph Byron. Dr. Byron is Chief Surgeon at the City of Hope Cancer Hospital in Los Angeles. My wife and I inaugurated this method with a slight modification and have found it to be a tremendous blessing. Here is how it works: each night one person leads the prayer time by praying for one subject at a time. The other partner then prays for the same subject. The first one then prays for the next burden of his heart and his partner again prays for the same thing. This procedure is continued until they have prayed for several things. The next night it is the other partner's turn to initiate prayer concerns, and by praying specifically for the burden of the other person's heart it isn't long before they are both burdened for the same thing. My wife and I found that after a few weeks we couldn't always remember who had the burden first, but came to identify ourselves with each other's burdens. Another blessing we discovered was that in prayer we were reminded to share things that we had forgotten to share because of the busy activities of the day. This sharing further broadens the bond between a husband and wife.

Having reached a stalemate with two of the couples I was counseling, I decided to ask them to try this method of prayer. One couple started that very night, and within a week called to say they didn't feel they needed to come in for counseling any more because "the Lord has solved our difficulties." The other couple refused to enter into this prayer relationship and though many months have passed it is quite apparent they are still living in an "armed truce."

Someone has said, "You can't quarrel with the woman you have prayed with every day." There is something humbling about getting down on your knees together; it is emotionally beneficial to both parties. Many a couple has acknowledged they rise from their knees more genuinely intertwined than before they prayed. Try it and see.

Who should initiate prayer? Ordinarily the husband, the head of the home; but if he doesn't, the wife may. Both must desire prayer for it to be a mutual help. The time spent in prayer together can very well be the most valuable time of your lives. Don't wait until the complexities of life drive you to your knees. If you wait until some difficulty arises to pray together, you will find that when you need God most you know him least. Learn to know him together in prayer now so that when life's pressure is on, you can go in prayer to one you have already learned to know as a close friend.

Key of Christ

"Things equal to the same thing are equal to each other" is a well-known geometric principle. If two people are properly related in a personal way to Jesus Christ, they will most likely be properly related to each other. *Jesus Christ wants to be Lord and Savior of you as an individual, then he wants to be the Lord of your marriage.* If he is, then the home you are building will abide in lasting peace and blessing. If he is not the spiritual head of your home, you will find that you will never experience all of the blessing that God has for you in marriage. Jesus said, "Without me ye can do nothing" (John 15:5).

If you have never received Jesus Christ, may I suggest that right now you bow your head and invite him into your life. He said, "Behold, I stand at the door, and knock: if any man hear my voice, and open the door, I will come in to him, and will sup with him, and he with me" (Revelation 3:20). If you desire him to come into your life, all you need do is ask him. Once inside, he will direct you by his Spirit in all areas of life and will "supply all your need."

The test of all marital behavior in relationship to Christ should be, "Is it done with his approval?" The Scripture teaches, "And whatsoever ye do in word or deed, do all in the name of the Lord Jesus, giving thanks to God and the Father by him" (Colossians 3:17). Jesus Christ is interested in every area of your life: physical, emotional, financial, and spiritual. Living in accordance with his will as revealed in the Bible is the most important thing you can do to insure a happy marriage. You can then say:

Christ is the head of this house,
The unseen guest at every meal,
The silent listener to every conversation.

Without a doubt, *Christ* is the greatest key to happiness in marriage.

If you constantly ask God to help you use these six keys in your marriage, your home will become increasingly happy and fulfilling.

○ ○ ○